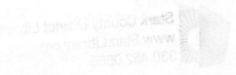

Table of Contents

Rourke
Educational Media
rourkeeducationalmedia.com

Can you find these words?

chlorophyll

fall

leaves

sunlight

Leaves Fall

leaves

Leaves make food for a tree.

Chlorophyll captures **sunlight**.

Leaves are green because of chlorophyll.

sunlight

Chlorophyll helps make food for the tree.

In autumn, days are short and cold. Leaves can't make food.

7

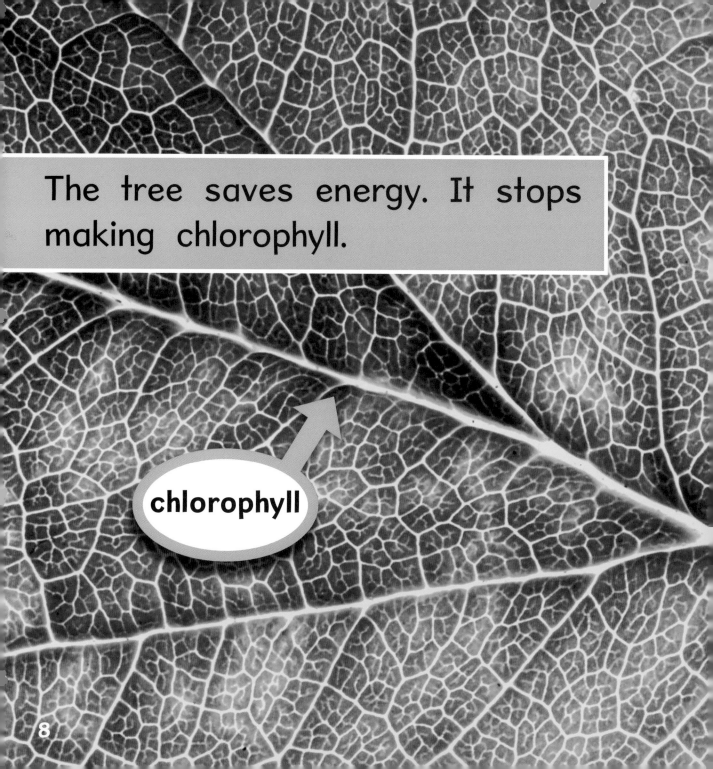

The tree saves energy. It stops making chlorophyll.

chlorophyll

It loses its leaves.

9

Leaves **fall** off the tree.

New leaves will grow in the spring.

Did you find these words?

Leaves are green because of **chlorophyll.**

Leaves **fall** off the tree.

Leaves make food for a tree.

Chlorophyll captures **sunlight**.

Photo Glossary

 **chlorophyll** (KLOR-uh-fil): The green substance in plants that uses light to make food.

 **fall** (fawl): To drop from a higher place to a lower place.

 **leaves** (leevs): Flat, usually green structures attached to a stem that grows from a tree or plant.

 **sunlight** (SUHN-lite): The light of the sun.

Index

About the Author

Lisa K. Schnell writes books for children. She also likes to dance, make art, and collect beautiful leaves.

www.rourkeeducationalmedia.com

PHOTO CREDITS: Cover: ©skynesher; p. 2,8,14,15: ©MLiberra; p. 2,10,14,15: ©Smileus; p. 2,3,14,15: ©XiXinXing; p. 2,4,14,15: ©Borut Trdina; p. 5: ©Jasmina007; p. 6: ©Michael Ver Sprill; p. 12: ©Borut Trdina.

Edited by: Keli Sipperley
Cover design by: Kathy Walsh
Interior design by: Rhea Magaro-Wallace

Library of Congress PCN Data
Leaves Fall / Lisa K. Schnell
(I Know)
ISBN (hard cover)(alk. paper) 978-1-64156-169-3
ISBN (soft cover) 978-1-64156-225-6
ISBN (e-Book) 978-1-64156-278-2
Library of Congress Control Number:2017957779

Printed in the United States of America, North Mankato, Minnesota